LEARNING ENGLISH *with* ANIMATIONS
만화영화로 배우는 영어

LEARNING ENGLISH with ANIMATIONS

만화영화로 배우는 영어 ___ 이영주 편저

도서출판 동인

TABLE OF CONTENTs

7 About Sexism

9 Snow White

23 Sleeping Beauty

37 The Little Mermaid

51 Beauty and the Beast

65 The Nightmare Before Christmas

83 Mulan

101 Shrek

115 Answers

About Sexism

Sexism is any attitudes and behaviours towards people that judge or belittle them on the basis of their **sex(gender)** [1] or that perpetuate stereotypical assumptions about sex(gender) roles. The term is most often used to refer to men's attitudes towards women, although in recent years there has been increasing discussion of sexism by women towards men.

The words gender and sex are often used interchangeably, but sex relates specifically to the biological, physical characteristics which make a person male or female at birth, whereas gender refers to the behaviours associated with members of that sex.

... History

While the term "sexism" dates from the mid-1960s and came into frequent use after the rise of women's liberation movements in 1968-1969, the practice of sexism has a long history.

Many of the predominant cultures in the world today were founded on a **patriarchal system** [2] (rule by fathers). The religions of Christianity, Judaism, Islam, Hinduism, and Confucianism—which together cover much of Europe, the Americas, North Africa, the Middle East, India, and China—have all produced patriarchal cultures.

Traditionally, rights to property and nationality passed through the male line, with the result that women's legal status was generally inferior to that of men: until the 20th century, women had no voting rights, limited rights to

> **1. Gender** : the sex-role identity used by humans to emphasize the distinctions between males and females.
> **2. Patriarchal system** is a form of social organization in which a male is the family head and title is traced through the male line.

property, and were, in most respects, subject entirely to their fathers or husbands.

In the 20th century, activists in many parts of the world have achieved a steady improvement in women's legal rights. Change has happened more slowly in Eastern cultures, where practices such as purdah (the confinement of women to the home), female circumcision, the killing of female children, and the husband's privileged right to divorceial are still found. Legal reform in some states has sought to improve women's position; India, for example, has made reforms to combat purdah.

Feminists in Eastern countries have also appealed to the United Nations to enforce women's rights. In the West, discussion has shifted from legal rights towards attacking prevailing sexist attitudes in society; authors Virginia Woolf and Simone de Beauvoir were among the earlier exponents. The women's and gay liberation movements which emerged particularly in Britain and the United States in the late 1960s also succeeded in raising public consciousness about sexism.

More recently, the issue of sexism against men has come into public debate in the writings. An important issue has been men's lack of rights, particularly those relating to child custody.

Snow White ...1937

Summary...... A long time ago, a child was born to a queen and king and she was called Snow White. When the queen died, the king married again. But the new queen was wicked and hated Snow White so much that she gave orders that Snow White was to be treated as a servant.

Snow White grew very beautiful and one day a Prince riding by, saw her at work and fell in love with her. But when the Queen consulted her Magic Mirror to find out that Snow White's beauty surpassed even her own, she ordered a hunter to kill Snow White. However, the hunter couldn't kill Snow White and Snow White was forced to flee into the forest, where she befriended seven dwarfs to cook and look after them.

Soon the Queen discovered Snow White was alive and also where Snow White was living. So the Queen disguised herself as a witch, took a poisoned apple and set out for the Dwarfs' cottage. She gave Snow White the poisoned apple to eat and as soon as she bit the apple, she sank into unconsciousness.

Thinking she was dead, the Dwarfs built a glass coffin and put her in it. For days she lay in the forest in her glass coffin. One day, the Prince was riding through the forest looking for Snow White and found her. He kissed her and then she opened her eyes. The Prince took Snow White to his palace where they were married and lived happily ever after.

1. Who is the Fairest of All?

SCORE

... Queen :

Magic ¹_____ on the ²_____ , who is the ³_____ one of all?

... Magic Mirror :

Famed is thy ⁴_____ , Majesty. ⁵_____ hold, a lovely maid I ⁶_____ . Rags cannot ⁷_____ her gentle ⁸_____ . Alas, ⁹_____ is more ¹⁰_____ than ¹¹_____ .

... Queen :

¹²_____ for her! ¹³_____ her ¹⁴_____ .

... Magic Mirror :

¹⁵_____ red as the ¹⁶_____ . ¹⁷_____ ¹⁸_____ as ebony. ¹⁹_____ white as ²⁰_____ .

... Queen :

Snow ²¹_____ !

EXAMPLEs

alas beauty black but fair fairest grace hair hide lips mirror
name reveal rose see she skin snow thee wall white

WORDs and IDIOMs

- thy [ðai] : pron. thou의 소유격, 너의 (=your)
- Majesty [mǽdʒəsti] : n. 폐하, 전하
- hold [hould] : vt. 기다리다, ~을 삼가다
- maid [meid] : n. 소녀, 아가씨
- rag [ræg] : n. 누더기, 넝마
- reveal [rivíːl] : vt. 밝히다
- ebony [ébəni] : n. 흑단나무

2. I'll Keep House for You.

SCORE

... **Small Dwarfs** :

Who, uh, who, who, who's butterin' like a spoodledug? Who's ru –

Uh, gutter – Aw, ¹_____ up and tell ²_____ to ³_____ out!

... **Snow White** :

Please ⁴_____ send me ⁵_____ ! ⁶_____ you do, she'll ⁷_____ me.

... **Small Dwarfs** :

⁸_____ you? Who will? Yes, who?

... **Snow White** :

My ⁹_____ , the Queen.

... **Small Dwarfs** :

The ¹⁰_____ ? She's wicked! She's bad! She's mighty mean!

She's an old ¹¹_____ ! I'm warnin' ya. If the Queen ¹²_____

her here, she'll swoop 13_____ and wreak her vengeance on us!

... **Snow White :**

But she doesn't 14_____ where I 15_____ !

... **Small Dwarf :**

She doesn't, eh? She 16_____ 17_____. She's full of black 18_____. She 19_____ even 20_____ herself 21_____. Might 22_____ in this 23_____ right 24_____.

... **Snow White :**

Oh, she'll 25_____ find 26_____ here. And if you let 27_____ stay, I'll 28_____ house for you. I'll 29_____ and sew and 30_____ and 31_____ and–

... **Small Dwarf :**

Cook? C-Can 32_____ make dapple lumpkins. Uh, lumple dapplings –

... **Small Dwarfs :**

33_____ dumplings!

... **Small Dwarf:**

Eh, yes! Crapple dumpkins.

… **Snow White :**

<u> ³⁴_____ </u>, and plum pudding and gooseberry <u> ³⁵_____ </u> –

… **Small Dwarfs :**

Gooseberry pie? Hooray! <u> ³⁶_____ </u> stays!

~ ~ ~ ♩ ♪ 🎵 ~ ~ ~

Ahh! <u> ³⁷_____ </u> ! Hurry. ~ ~ ~ Hooray

… **Snow White :**

Uh, uh, uh. Just a <u> ³⁸_____ </u> . Supper is <u> ³⁹_____ </u> quite <u> ⁴⁰_____ </u> . You will just <u> ⁴¹_____ </u> time to <u> ⁴²_____ </u> .

EXAMPLEs

am	apple	away	be	can	cook	don't	down	everything	finds
get	have	her	if	invisible	keep	kill	know	knows	magic	make
me	minute	never	not	now	pie	queen	ready	room	she	shut
soup	stepmother	sweep	wash	witch	yes	you

WORDs and IDIOMs

- butter [bʌ́tər] : vt. 아첨하다
- gutter [gʌ́tər] : n. 빈민굴, 하수도
- stepmother [stépmʌ̀ðəːr] : n. 계모

- wicked [wíkid] : a. 사악한
- witch [witʃ] : n. 마녀
- ya [jə] = you
- swoop [swu:p] : vi. 급습하다
- wreak [ri:k] : vt. ~에게 복수를 하다
- vengeance [véndʒəns] : n. 복수
- invisible [invízəbl] : a. 눈에 보이지 않는
- sew [sou] : v. 바느질하다
- sweep [swi:p] : v. 청소하다
- dapple [dǽpl] : a. 얼룩진, 얼룩배기의
  n. 얼룩, 얼룩배기
- dumpling [dʌ́mpliŋ] : n. 가루반죽 푸딩
- plum [plʌm] : n. 자두
- gooseberry [gú:sbèri] : n. 구스베리(의 열매)
- hooray [huréi] (hurrah=hoorah) : int. 만세, 만세를 부르다

3. A Love Story.

SCORE |

… **Small Dwarfs :**

Tell us a ¹_____ . Yes, tell ²_____ a ³_____ .

A ⁴_____ story. A ⁵_____ story.

… **Snow White :**

Well, ⁶_____ there was a princess.

… **Small Dwarf :**

Was ⁷_____ princess you?

… **Snow White :**

And she ⁸_____ in love…. Anyone ⁹_____ see that the

prince was ¹⁰_____ . The only ¹¹_____ for me.

… **Small Dwarfs :**

Was he, uh, uh, uh, ¹²_____ and handsome? Was he ¹³_____

and ¹⁴_____ ?

... **Snow White :**

There's ⁱ⁵_____ like him anywhere at ¹⁶_____ .

... **Small Dwarfs :**

Did he ¹⁷_____ he loved ya? Did he ¹⁸_____ a kiss?

... **Snow White :**

He was so ¹⁹_____ . I could ²⁰_____ resist.

~ ~ ~ ♩ ♪ ♫ ~ ~ ~

Someday my ²¹_____ will come. ²²_____ we'll ²³_____ again. And away to his ²⁴_____ we'll go to be happy ²⁵_____ .

EXAMPLEs

all big castle charming could fell forever love meet nobody
not once one prince romantic say someday steal story strong
tall the true us

WORDs and IDIOMs

• **charming** [tʃármiŋ] : a. 매력적인
• **handsome** [hǽnsəm] : a. 풍채 좋은, 잘생긴
• **steal** [sti:l] : vt. 훔치다   *steal a kiss : 슬쩍 키스하다
• **resist** [rizíst] : vt. ~에 저항하다, 참다
• **castle** [kǽsl] : n. 성

4. Magic Wishing Apple.

SCORE

... **Queen :**

'Cause you've been so ¹_____ to poor ²_____ granny,

I'll share a ³_____ with you. This is no ⁴_____ apple.

It's a ⁵_____ wishing ⁶_____ .

... **Snow White :**

A wishing ⁷_____ ?

... **Queen :**

Yes! One ⁸_____ and all your ⁹_____ will come

¹⁰_____ .

... **Snow White :**

Really?

... **Queen :**

Yes, girlie. Now, ¹¹_____ a wish... and ¹²_____ a bite...

There must be ¹³_____ your little heart ¹⁴_____ .

Perhaps there is 15_____ you 16_____ .

… **Snow White :**

Well, there is 17_____ .

… **Queen :**

I 18_____ so. I thought 19_____ ! Ho, ho ho ~ ~ Old granny 20_____ a young girl's 21_____ . Now, 22_____ the apple, dearie and make a 23_____ .

… **Snow White :**

I wish, I 24_____ –

… **Queen :**

That's it, 25_____ on! Go 26_____ .

~ ~ ~ ♩ ♪ ♫

… **Snow White :**

And that he will 27_____ me away to his 28_____ … where we will 29_____ happily ever 30_____ .

… **Queen :**

Fine! Fine! Now take a 31_____ .

~ ~ ♩ ♪ ♫ ~ ~

Don't let the wish grow 32_____ !

… **Snow White :**

Oh, I feel ³³_____ .

EXAMPLEs

after apple bite carry castle cold desires dreams go good
heart knows live love magic make old on ordinary secret
so someone something strange take thought true wish

WORDs and IDIOMs

- granny [grǽni] : n. 할머니
- secret [síːkrit] : n. 비밀
- ordinary [ɔ́ːrdənèri] : a. 평범한
- magic [mǽdʒik] : a. 마법의
- wishing [wíʃiŋ] : a. 소원을 비는   *make a wish : 소원을 빌다
- bite [bait] : vt. 한입 물다   *take a bite : 한입 먹다
- girlie [gə́ːrli] : n. 소녀, 아가씨
- dearie = deary [díəri] : 귀여운 사람
- cold [kould] : a. 김샌, 흥을 깨뜨리는

MEMO

Sleeping Beauty ...1959

Summary...... A long time ago, in a kingdom far away, King Stefan and the Queen have a daughter, Aurora. To celebrate the birth, all of the people in the kingdom went to the royal castle, bearing gifts for the princess. Also attending were the three good fairies, Flora, Fauna and Merryweather. Each came to give the princess one gift. Flora gave her the gift of beauty. Fauna gave the gift of song. But before Merryweather could bestow her gift, the evil Maleficent appeared.

Maleficent was angry that she had not been invited to the celebration. She curses Aurora, predicting that at the age of sixteen the princess will prick her finger on the spindle of a spinning-wheel and die. Merryweather tries to undo the damage by casting a spell that will allow the princess to awake from an ageless sleep with a kiss from her true love.

King Stefan, however, was still afraid for his daughter and ordered every spinning wheel in the kingdom to be burned. Moreover, fearing Maleficent's magic, the three fairies take Aurora to their cottage in the woods to keep her away from the eyes of Maleficent, and raise her as their own child, named Briar Rose.

On her 16th birthday Aurora meets Prince Phillip and falls in love. But Maleficent manages to kidnap the Prince and her horrible prophecy is fulfilled when she tricks Aurora into touching a spinning wheel created by Maleficent herself. Realizing that the Prince is in trouble, the fairies head to Maleficent's castle at the Forbidden Mountain, and spring the Prince loose.

But the Prince soon finds himself up against Maleficent's evil spells which include a thorn forest as thick as weeds around King Stefan's castle and a fight against Maleficent when she turns herself into a dragon. Finally the Prince manages to kill the dragon and then Maleficent's magic forest dissolves. So the Prince finds Aurora and kisses her to wake everyone as well as her up and to marry her.

1. A Princess Was Born.

SCORE |

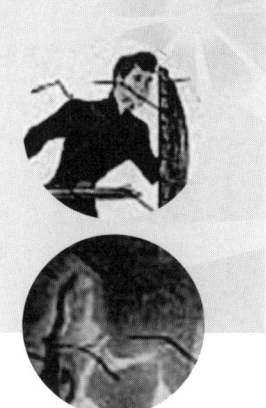

Narrator :

In a ¹_____ away ²_____ , long ³_____ , lived a ⁴_____ and his ⁵_____ queen. Many ⁶_____ had ⁷_____ longed ⁸_____ a ⁹_____ and ¹⁰_____ their ¹¹_____ was granted.

A ¹²_____ was ¹³_____ , and they ¹⁴_____ her Aurora.

~ ~ ♩ ♪ ♫ ~ ~

Yes, ¹⁵_____ named her ¹⁶_____ the ¹⁷_____ for she filled their ¹⁸_____ with ¹⁹_____ . Then a ²⁰_____ ²¹_____ was proclaimed ²²_____ the ²³_____ , so that ²⁴_____ of ²⁵_____ or low ²⁶_____ might ²⁷_____ homage ²⁸_____ the ²⁹_____ princess.

EXAMPLEs

after ago all born called child daughter dawn estate fair far finally for great high holiday infant king kingdom land lives pay sunshine they throughout to wish years

WORDs and IDIOMs

- fair [fɛər] : a. 아름다운, 예쁜
- long [lɔːŋ] : a. 열망하다 (for) 간절히 바라다
- grant [grænt] : vt. 들어주다, 승인하다
- dawn [dɔːn] : n. 새벽, 여명
- proclaim [prouklέim] : vt. 선언하다, 공포하다
- estate [istéit] : n. 지위, 신발, 토지
- homage [hámidʒ] : n. 신하로서의 예, 충성
    *pay homage to~ : ~에게 경의를 표하다, 신하의 예를 다하다
- infant [ínfənt] : n. 7세 미만의 유아

2. Three Gifts.

SCORE

... **Announcer :**

The ¹_____ honored ²_____ exalted ³_____ , the ⁴_____ ⁵_____ fairies. Mistress Flora, ⁶_____ Fauna, ⁷_____ mistress Merryweather.

~ ~ ♩ ♪ ♫

... **Fairies :**

Oh, ⁸_____ little ⁹_____ ! ¹⁰_____ Majesties!

... **Flora :**

Each of ¹¹_____ the ¹²_____ may ¹³_____ with a ¹⁴_____ gift. No ¹⁵_____ , no ¹⁶_____ .

Little ¹⁷_____ , my ¹⁸_____ shall ¹⁹_____ the ²⁰_____ of the ²¹_____ .

... **Choir :**

One gift, ²²_____ rare.

Full of 23_____ in her hair.

Lips that shame the 24_____ red 25_____ .

She'll walk with springtime wherever 26_____ goes.

... **Fauna:**

27_____ princess, my 28_____ 29_____ be the 30_____ of song.

... **Choir :**

One 31_____ , the gift of 32_____ .

Melody her whole life long.

The nightingale's her troubadour.

Bringing her sweet serenade to her door.

... **Merryweather :**

33_____ princess, 34_____ 35_____ shall be…

(A blow of the wind.)

EXAMPLEs

and be beauty bless child darling excellencies gift good less
mistress more most my princess red rose shall she single
song sunshine sweet the three tiny us your

WORDs and IDIOMs

- honored [ánərd] : a. 명예로운
- exalt [igzɔ́:lt] : vt. 명예, 품위 따위를 높이다, 신분을 올리다.
- Excellencies : Excellency[éksələnsi]의 복수 : 각하, 부인
- fairies [fɛ́əriz] : fairy [fɛ́əri]의 복수 n. 요정
- Majesty [mǽdʒisti] : n. 폐하
- rare [rɛəːr] : a. 진기한
- troubadour [trúːbədɔr] : n. 음유시인
- serenade [sèrənéid] : n. 소야곡, 남자가 밤에 연인의 창 밑에서 부르는 노래

3. She Will Die.

SCORE |

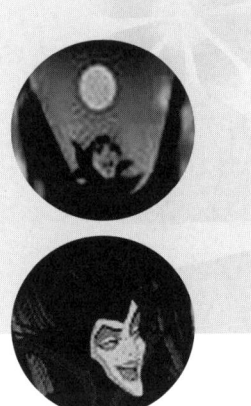

(Lightning and thunder)

... **Flora :**

Why, it's Maleficent!

... **Merryweather :**

What does ¹_____ want ²_____ ?

... **Fauna :**

Shhh!

... **Maleficent :**

Well, ³_____ a glittering assemblage, ⁴_____ Stefan.

⁵_____ , nobility, the ⁶_____ and, ⁷_____ quaint,

⁸_____ the rebel.

I ⁹_____ felt quite distressed of ¹⁰_____ ¹¹_____

an ¹²_____ .

... **Merryweather :**

You weren't wanted!

... **Maleficent :**

Not what…? Oh ¹³_____ , what an ¹⁴_____ ¹⁵_____ .

I had hoped ¹⁶_____ was merely due to some ¹⁷_____ .

Well, in that event I'd best be on my ¹⁸_____ .

... **Queen:**

And you're ¹⁹_____ offended, your ²⁰_____ ?

... **Maleficent :**

Why no, your ²¹_____ . And to ²²_____ I bear no ill ²³_____ , I too, ²⁴_____ bestow a ²⁵_____ on the ²⁶_____ . Listen ²⁷_____ , all of ²⁸_____ ! The ²⁹_____ shall indeed ³⁰_____ in ³¹_____ and ³²_____ , beloved ³³_____ all who ³⁴_____ her. ³⁵_____ , ³⁶_____ the sun ³⁷_____ on her sixteenth ³⁸_____ , she ³⁹_____ prick her ⁴⁰_____ ⁴¹_____ the spindle of a spinning ⁴²_____ and ⁴³_____ .

... **Queen :**

Oh ⁴⁴_____ !

SLEEPING BEAUTY 31

... Maleficent :

Ha, ha, ha, ha!

... Stefan :

Seize that ⁴⁵_____ !

... Maleficent :

Stand ⁴⁶_____ you ⁴⁷_____ . Aha ha ha ~ ~ ~ .

EXAMPLEs

awkward   back   beauty   before   birthday   but   by   child   creature
dear   die   even   excellency   finger   fool   gentry   gift   grace   grow
here   how   invitation   it   king   know   majesty   no   not   on   oversight
princess   quite   really   receiving   royalty   sets   shall   she   show
situation   way   well   wheel   will   you

WORDs and IDIOMs

- glitter [glítər] : vi. 빛나다, 반짝이다
- assemblage [əsémblidʒ] : n. 모인 사람들, 집단
- loyalty [lɔ́iəlti] : n. 충성
- nobility [noubíləti] : n. 귀족
- gentry [dʒéntri] : n. 상류 사회 사람들(귀족과 향사 사이의 계급)
- quaint [kweint] : a. 이상한, 기인한
- rebel [rébəl] : n. 반역자, 모반자
- distressed [distrésd] : a. 기분이 안 좋음, 걱정임, 괴로움

- awkward [ɔ́:kwərd] : a. 어색한, 거북한
- due [djú:] : a. ~의 탓으로 돌려야 할   *due to : ~ 때문에
- oversight [óuvərsàit] : n. 빠뜨림, 못 봄
- offended [əféndid] : a. 불쾌한, 기분이 상한
- bear [bɛər] : vt. 마음에 품다, 지니다
- bestow [bistóu] : vt. 주다, 수여하다
- grace [greis] : n. 품위, 우아함
- prick [prik] : v. (바늘로) 찌르다
- spindle [spíndl] : n. 물레의 가락 (실을 자아감는 토리구실을 하는 막대기)
- spinning [spíniŋ] : a. 방적의
- wheel [hwi:l] : n. 수레바퀴
- seize [si:z] : vt. 붙잡다, 체포하다

4. Not in Death, but in Sleep.

SCORE

... **Flora :**

Don't ¹_____ , your Majesties. Merryweather still ²_____ her ³_____ to ⁴_____ .

... **Stefan :**

Then ⁵_____ can undo ⁶_____ fearful ⁷_____ ?

... **Merryweather :**

Oh ⁸_____ , sire.

... **Flora :**

Maleficent's powers are ⁹_____ too ¹⁰_____ .

... **Fauna :**

But ¹¹_____ can ¹²_____ !

... **Merryweather :**

But ...

... **Fauna :**

Just ¹³_____ your ¹⁴_____ , dear.

... **Flora :**

Yes ...

... **Merryweather :**

Sweet ¹⁵_____ , if through this ¹⁶_____ witch's trick ¹⁷_____ spindle should your ¹⁸_____ prick, a ray of ¹⁹_____ there ²⁰_____ may be ²¹_____ this. The ²²_____ I give at thee. Not ²³_____ death but just in ²⁴_____ the fateful prophecy you'll ²⁵_____ , and ²⁶_____ this slumber you ²⁷_____ ²⁸_____ when true love's kiss the ²⁹_____ shall ³⁰_____ .

... **Choir :**

For true love conquers ³¹_____ .

— **EXAMPLEs**

a all best break curse despair do far finger from gift give great has help hope in keep no princess shall she sleep spell still this wake wicked

WORDs and IDIOMs

- undo [ʌndú] : vt. 원상태로 돌리다, 취소하다
- fearful [fíərfəl] : a. 무서운, 무시무시한
- curse [kə:rs] : n. 저주
- sire [saiə:r] : n. 폐하, 전하
- maleficent [məléfəsnt] : a. 유해한, 나쁜
- trick [trik] : n. 요술, 장난
- ray [rei] : n. (희망의) 빛
- fateful [féitfəl] : a. 결정적인, 중대한
- prophecy [práfəsi] : n. 예언
- slumber [slʌ́mbə:r] : n. 잠
- spell [spel] : n. 주문, 마력
- conquer [káŋkər] : vt. 정복하다, 극복하다, ~을 이겨내다

The Little Mermaid ...1989

Summary...... "The Little Mermaid" is a story about a mermaid named Ariel who longs to explore the world of human beings and also wants to become a human. One day when Ariel went to the surface, she saw a sailor named Prince Eric and saved his life to fall in love with him.

When her father King Triton learned of this, he destroyed the girl's collection of human artifacts and restricted her from seeing the prince again. However, Ariel struck a bargain with Ursula, the sea witch, agreeing to trade her voice for a pair of human legs. As with all bargains, this one comes with a catch: if Ariel can't score a kiss from her human love within two days,

Ursula will own her soul forever.

Prince Eric saw Ariel on the beach and took her back to his palace. Over the next few days Prince Eric grew to like Ariel more and more, but he had no way of identifying her as the woman who had saved his life. To make matters worse, Ursula assumed a human form of her own, using Ariel's voice to steal the Prince's heart and to marry him. But Ariel's sea gull friend Scuttle stalled the wedding and got Ariel's voice back for her.

When Eric realized it was Ariel that could sing so beautifully, he went to kiss her. But it was too late. Ariel was turned back into a mermaid. Prince Eric went to save Ariel from the sea witch and he killed her with his boat. Once King Triton realized how much Ariel loved this prince, he turned her back into a human. Ariel and the Prince got married that day and lived happily ever after.

1. He's So Handsome.

SCORE

... **Ariel :**

I've never ¹_____ a ²_____ this ³_____ ⁴_____ .

Oh, he's very ⁵_____ , ⁶_____ he?

... **Scuttle :**

I don't know. He looks like ⁷_____ and slobbery ⁸_____ me.

... **Ariel :**

Not ⁹_____ one, the one ¹⁰_____ the snarfblatt.

... **Grimsby :**

It isn't me ¹¹_____ . The ¹²_____ kingdom ¹³_____ to see ¹⁴_____ ¹⁵_____ settled ¹⁶_____ ... with the right girl.

... **Eric :**

She's ¹⁷_____ there ¹⁸_____ . I ¹⁹_____ ~

I ²⁰_____ haven't ²¹_____ her yet.

... **Grimsby** :

Perhaps ²²_____ haven't been ²³_____ hard ²⁴_____ .

... **Eric** :

Believe ²⁵_____ . When I ²⁶_____ her, I'll know, without a doubt. It'll just ²⁷_____ me, like ²⁸_____ .

EXAMPLEs

alone   before   close   down   enough   entire   find   found   hairy
handsome   happily   hit   human   isn't   just   lightning   looking   me   out
playing   seen   somewhere   that   to   wants   you

WORDs and IDIOMs

- hairy [hέəri] : a. 털투성이의, 덥수룩한
- slobbery [slábəri] : a. 단정치 못한
- entire [entáiər] : a. 전체의
- settle [sétl] : vi. 정착하다, 자리를 잡다

2. What Would I Give?

SCORE

... **Ariel :**

Is he… ¹_____ ?

... **Scuttle :**

It's ²_____ to ³_____ . Oh, I, I can't ⁴_____ out a ⁵_____ .

... **Ariel :**

No, look! He's ⁶_____ . He's ⁷_____ ⁸_____ .

... **Song (Ariel) :**

⁹_____ would I ¹⁰_____ to ¹¹_____ where you are?

¹²_____ would I ¹³_____ to ¹⁴_____ here ¹⁵_____ ¹⁶_____ ?

What ¹⁷_____ I do to ¹⁸_____ you ¹⁹_____ ²⁰_____ me?

Where would we walk?

21_____ we run if we 22_____ 23_____ all day in the 24_____ ?

Just 25_____ and 26_____ .

And I 27_____ be 28_____ of your 29_____ .

EXAMPLEs

at beautiful beside breathing could dead give hard heartbeat
live make me part pay say see smiling so stay sun what
where world would you

WORDs and IDIOMs

- heartbeat[háːrtbiːt] : n. 심장박동
- breathe [briːð] : v. 숨을 쉬다

3. I'll Swim to His Castle.

SCORE

... **Ariel :**

He ¹_____ me. He loves ²_____ ³_____ .

⁴_____ loves ⁵_____ ! Aha, ha, ha. I ⁶_____ it!

... **Sebastian :**

Ariel, ⁷_____ talking ⁸_____ !

... **Ariel :**

I've ⁹_____ ¹⁰_____ see him ¹¹_____ . Scuttle knows

¹²_____ he ¹³_____ .

... **Sebastian :**

Ariel, please, ¹⁴_____ you ¹⁵_____ your ¹⁶_____ out of

the ¹⁷_____ ... and back ¹⁸_____ the ¹⁹_____ where it

²⁰_____ .

... **Ariel :**

I'll ²¹_____ to his ²²_____ . Then Flounder will ²³_____

THE LITTLE MERMAID 43

to ²⁴_____ his ²⁵_____ .

... **Sebastian :**

Down ²⁶_____ is your ²⁷_____ !

— **EXAMPLEs** —

attention belongs castle clouds crazy get got he head here
home in knew loves me not splash stop swim to tonight
water where will

WORDs and IDIOMs

- cloud [klaud] : n. 공상 *have one's head in the clouds : 공상에 잠기다
- splash [splæʃ] : vt. 물을 튀기다
- attention [əténʃən] : n. 주의

4. I Love Him.

SCORE |

... **Triton :**

You ¹_____ a ²_____ from ³_____ ?

... **Ariel :**

Daddy, ⁴_____ had to.

... **Triton :**

Contact between the ⁵_____ and mer ⁶_____ is strictly

⁷_____ . Ariel, ⁸_____ know ⁹_____ ! Everyone

¹⁰_____ that!

... **Ariel :**

He ¹¹_____ have ¹²_____ .

... **Triton :**

One ¹³_____ human to ¹⁴_____ ¹⁵_____ .

... **Ariel :**

You ¹⁶_____ ¹⁷_____ him.

THE LITTLE MERMAID

... Triton :

Know him? I ⁱ⁸_____ have to ¹⁹_____ him. They're ²⁰_____ the ²¹_____ spineless, ²²_____, harpooning ²³_____ -eaters. ²⁴_____ of any ²⁵_____ !

... Ariel :

Daddy I ²⁶_____ ²⁷_____ !

... Triton :

²⁸_____ . Have you ²⁹_____ your ³⁰_____ completely? ³¹_____ 's a ³²_____ . ³³_____ a ³⁴_____ .

... Ariel :

³⁵_____ don't ³⁶_____ .

... Triton :

So ³⁷_____ me, Ariel. I am ³⁸_____ to got ³⁹_____ to you. If ⁴⁰_____ is ⁴¹_____ ⁴²_____ way, ⁴³_____ be it!

... Ariel :

Daddy! ⁴⁴_____ ! Don't! Please! Daddy, stop! Daddy, ⁴⁵_____ it! ⁴⁶_____ , no!

EXAMPLEs

about all care daddy died don't drowning feeling fish forbidden going he's help him human I incapable know knows less lost love mermaid no only rescued same savage senses so stop that the this through world worry would you you're

 **WORDs and IDIOMs**

- rescue [réskju:] : vt. 구조하다
- drown [draun] : vt. 익사하다
- contact [kántæt] : n. 접촉
- strictly [strítli] : adv. 엄격히
- forbidden [fəːrbídn] : forbid [fəːrbíd]의 과거분사. vt. 금지하다
- spineless [spáinlis] : a. 지느러미 가시가 없는, 용기 없는
- savage [sǽvidʒ] : n. 야만인, 미개인, 잔인한 사람
- harpoon [hɑːrpúːn] : vt. ~을 작살로 잡다
- incapable [inkéipəbəl] : a. ~을 할 수 없는
- mermaid [mə́ːrmèid] : n. 인어

5. Never Be with My Family Again?

SCORE

... **Ursula :**

Have we ¹_____ a ²_____ ?

... **Ariel :**

If I ³_____ a ⁴_____ , I'll ⁵_____ be ⁶_____ my

⁷_____ or ⁸_____ ⁹_____ .

... **Ursula :**

That's ¹⁰_____ . ¹¹_____ you'll ¹²_____ your ¹³_____ .

¹⁴_____ 's ¹⁵_____ of tough ¹⁶_____ , isn't ¹⁷_____ ?

Oh, ¹⁸_____ ¹⁹_____ is one ²⁰_____ ²¹_____ .

²²_____ haven't ²³_____ the ²⁴_____ of ²⁵_____ .

You can't ²⁶_____ ²⁷_____ for ²⁸_____ , you ²⁹_____ .

... **Ariel :**

But I ³⁰_____ ...

... **Ursula :**

I'm not ³¹_____ much, just a ³²_____, a ³³_____. ³⁴_____ 'll never ³⁵_____ ³⁶_____. ³⁷_____ I ³⁸_____ from ³⁹_____ is, your ⁴⁰_____.

... **Ariel :**

My ⁴¹_____ ?

... **Ursula :**

⁴²_____ 've ⁴³_____ it, sweetcakes. No ⁴⁴_____, ⁴⁵_____, ⁴⁶_____, zip.

... **Ariel :**

But ⁴⁷_____ ⁴⁸_____ voice, ⁴⁹_____ can I…

... **Ursula :**

You'll ⁵⁰_____ your ⁵¹_____, your ⁵²_____ ⁵³_____, and ⁵⁴_____ underestimate the ⁵⁵_____ of … ⁵⁶_____ ⁵⁷_____ ! Ha! The ⁵⁸_____ up there ⁵⁹_____ ⁶⁰_____ a lot blabber they ⁶¹_____ a girl who ⁶²_____ is a bore, yes, on ⁶³_____ it's much preferred for ⁶⁴_____ ⁶⁵_____ to say a ⁶⁶_____ .

EXAMPLEs

again and asking become body but choices deal discussed don't face father full get gossips got have how human importance it know ladies land language life like looks man men miss more my never not nothing payment pretty right singing sisters something subject talking there thing think token trifle voice want we what with without word you you'll

WORDs and IDIOMs

- deal [di:l] : n. 거래
- tough [tʌf] : a. 곤란한, 힘든
- discuss [diskʌ́s] : vt. ~을 논의하다
- payment [péimənt] : n. 보상
- token [tóukən] : n. 표시
- trifle [traifl] : n. 하찮은 것, 시시한 것
- zip [zip] : n. 지퍼   vt. ~을 지퍼로 잠그다
- looks [luks] : n. (보통 ~s) 얼굴, 외관, 용모, 외모
- underestimate [ʌ̀ndəréstəmèit] : v. 과소평가하다, 경시하다
- gossip [gásip] : n. 뜬소문, 험담
- blabber [blǽbər] : n. 수다장이
- bore [bo:r] : n. 귀찮은 사람, 성가신 사람
- prefer [prifə́:r] : vt. ~을 좋아하다

Beauty and the Beast ...1991

Summary...... Once upon a time a poor merchant lived in a small home with his daughter. One night during a storm, a poor merchant takes shelter in a magical castle. In the morning as he leaves, he plucks a rose as a gift for his daughter. When he does so, a monstrous beast appears and threatens his life. The merchant can leave unharmed only after he promises to send his daughter to the beast instead. He does so, and while she is at first terrified of the creature she soon learns he is kind and gentle.

Every night, however, the beast asks her to marry him and every night she says no. Although she is not supposed to leave the castle, the beast gives her permission to do so when she learns her father is dying, under the condition that she returns within a specified amount of time. However, she stays away longer, and when she returns she finds the beast collapsed and apparently dead. She then weeps and says she loves him, at which point he comes back to life and is transformed into a prince, who had been under enchantment until someone should love him despite his appearance.

1. Belle Is a Funny Girl.

SCORE |

... **Baker :**

Good ¹_____ , Belle!

... **Belle :**

²_____ _____ Monsieur!

... **Baker :**

Where are ³_____ off ⁴_____ ?

... **Belle :**

The ⁵_____ ! I just ⁶_____ the most ⁷_____ story, ⁸_____ a beanstalk ⁹_____ an ogre and …

... **Baker :**

That's ¹⁰_____ … Marie, the baguettes! ¹¹_____ ¹²_____ !!

... **Townsfolk :**

¹³_____ there ¹⁴_____ goes, that ¹⁵_____ is

¹⁶_____ no ¹⁷_____ . Dazed and distracted, ¹⁸_____ you ¹⁹_____ ?

... **Woman 1 :**

Never part of any ²⁰_____ .

... **Barber :**

Cause her head's up on ²¹_____ cloud.

... **Townsfolk :**

No denying ²²_____ a ²³_____ girl, that Belle!

EXAMPLEs

about   and   bookshop   can't   crowd   finished   funny   girl   hurry   look   morning   nice   question   she   she's   some   strange   tell   to   up   wonderful   you

---

WORDs and IDIOMs

- monsieur [məsjɔ́ːr] : n. ~씨, ~님
- bookshop[búkʃːɑp] : n. 책방, 서점
- beanstalk [bíːnstɔ̀ːk] : n. 콩줄기
- ogre [óugər] : n. 사람 잡아먹는 귀신, 괴물
- baguette [bæɡét] : n. 막대 모양으로 생긴 프랑스 빵
- dazed [deizd] : a. 멍한
- distracted [distrǽktid] : a. 마음을 딴 데로 돌린

- crowd [kraud] : n. 군중, 대중
- deny [dinaí] : vt. 부인하다, 부정하다
- funny [fʌ́ni] : a. 재미있는, 우스운

2. Belle's Favorite Book.

SCORE

... **Belle :**

Good morning. I've come to ¹_____ the book I ²_____ .

... **Bookseller :**

Finished ³_____ ?

... **Belle :**

Oh, I couldn't ⁴_____ it down! Have you ⁵_____ anything ⁶_____ ?

... **Bookseller :**

Ha, ha. Not ⁷_____ yesterday.

... **Belle :**

⁸_____ all ⁹_____ . I'll ¹⁰_____ ... ¹¹_____ one.

... **Bookseller :**

That one? But you've ¹²_____ it twice!

... **Belle :**

Well it's my ¹³_____ ! ¹⁴_____ off places, daring sword fights, ¹⁵_____ spells, a ¹⁶_____ in disguise!

... **Bookseller :**

Well, if you ¹⁷_____ it all that much, it's ¹⁸_____ !

... **Belle :**

But sir!

... **Bookseller :**

I ¹⁹_____ !

... **Belle :**

Well ²⁰_____ you. Thank ²¹_____ ²²_____ much!

... **Men :**

Look there ²³_____ goes. That girl is so ²⁴_____ !

I ²⁵_____ if she's feeling well!

... **Women :**

With a ²⁶_____ far-off look!

... **Men :**

And ²⁷_____ nose stuck in a ²⁸_____ !

... All :

What ²⁹_____ puzzle ³⁰_____ the rest of ³¹_____ is Belle!

EXAMPLEs

a already book borrow(ed) dreamy far favorite feeling got her
insist like magic new peculiar prince put read return right she
since thank that's this to us very wonder you yours

WORDs and IDIOMs

- borrow[bárou] : vt. 빌리다
- daring [déəriŋ] : a. 대담한, 용감한
- magic [mǽdʒik] : n. 마술
- spell [spel] : n. 주문, 마력
- disguise [disgáiz] : n. 변장, 분장
- insist [insíst] : v. 고집하다, 끝까지 주장하다
- peculiar [pikjú:ljər] : a. 독특한, 별난
- dreamy [drí:mi] : a. 공상에 잠기는, 어렴풋한
- far-off [fá:r-ɔ́:f] : a. 멀리 떨어진, 아득한 옛날의
- stuck [stʌk] : stick [stik]의 과거, 과거분사. vt. 빠져서 움직이지 않게 하다, 들러붙게 하다
- puzzle [pʌ́zl] : n. 수수께끼

3. Different from the Rest of Us.

SCORE

... **Belle :**

Oh! ¹_____ this ²_____ ! ³_____ my ⁴_____ part ⁵_____ , you'll ⁶_____ ! ⁷_____ where ⁸_____ meets ⁹_____ Charming. But ¹⁰_____ won't ¹¹_____ that it's ¹²_____ 'til chapter ¹³_____ !

... **Woman 5 :**

Now ¹⁴_____ no ¹⁵_____ ¹⁶_____ her ¹⁷_____ means ¹⁸_____ . Her ¹⁹_____ have got ²⁰_____ parallel!

... **Merchant :**

But ²¹_____ that ²²_____ facade. I'm ²³_____ she's rather ²⁴_____ . Very ²⁵_____ from the ²⁶_____ of us ...

... **All :**

She's ²⁷_____ like the rest of us. Yes ²⁸_____ from the

²⁹_____ of ³⁰_____ is Belle.

EXAMPLEs

afraid amazing beauty because behind different discover fair
favorite here's him isn't it's looks name no nothing odd prince
rest see she that three us wonder

WORDs and IDIOMs

- amazing [əméiziŋ] : a. 놀랄 정도의, 굉장한
- behind [biháind] : ad. 뒤에, 이면에
- parallel [pǽrəlèl] : a. 견줄만한, 유사한
- fair [fɛər] 아름다운, 매력적인
- facade [fəsá:d] : n. 외관

4. He's Not for Me.

SCORE

... **Maurice :**

So, ¹_____ you have a good ²_____ in town today?

... **Belle :**

I got a new ³_____ . Papa, do you think I'm ⁴_____ ?

... **Maurice :**

My daughter? ⁵_____ ? Where would ⁶_____ get an ⁷_____ like that?

... **Belle :**

Oh, I ⁸_____ know. It's just that I'm not ⁹_____ I ¹⁰_____ in here. There's no ¹¹_____ I can really talk ¹²_____ .

... **Maurice :**

What ¹³_____ that Gaston? He's a ¹⁴_____ fellow!

... **Belle** :

He's ¹⁵_____ all ¹⁶_____, and ¹⁷_____ and conceited and … Oh Papa, he's not ¹⁸_____ me!

EXAMPLEs

about   book   did   don't   fit   for   handsome   idea   odd   one   right
rude   sure   time   to   you

WORDs and IDIOMs

- odd [ɑd/ɔd] : a. 이상한, 기묘한, 색다른
- fit [fit] : v. ~에 어울리다, 맞다
- fellow [félou] : n. 친구, 동무, 사람, 녀석
- rude [ru:d] : a. 무례한, 버릇없는
- conceited [kənsíːtid] : a. 자만심이 강한, 우쭐한, 젠체하는

5. There's Something in Him.

SCORE

Belle :

There's something ¹_____ . And almost ²_____ . But he was ³_____ . and he was coarse ⁴_____ unrefined. And now he's ⁵_____ and so ⁶_____ . I wonder ⁷_____ I didn't see it ⁸_____ before.

. . .

New, and a bit ⁹_____ . Who'd have ever ¹⁰_____ that this could be? True, that he's no Prince ¹¹_____ . But there's ¹²_____ in him that I ¹³_____ didn't see.

EXAMPLEs

alarming   and   charming   dear   kind   mean   simply   something
sweet   there   thought   unsure   why

WORDs and IDIOMs

- mean [miːn] : a. 심술궂은 하잘 것 없는, 비열한
- coarse [kɔːrs] : a. 야비한
- unrefined [ʌ̀nrifáind] : a. 세련되지 않은, 촌스러운
- unsure [ʌnʃúər] : a. 불안정한, 신용할 수 없는
- bit [bit] : n. 조금   *a bit : 약간, 조금
- alarming [əlάːrmiŋ] : a. 놀라운
- simply [símpli] : ad. 전혀(absolutely), 정말

The Nightmare Before Christmas ...1993

Summary...... Tim Burton's "Nightmare Before Christmas" started as a poem Tim Burton wrote while working as an animator at Disney in the early '80s. "The Nightmare Before Christmas" then became the first full-length stop-motion animated film ever created.

In "The Nightmare Before Christmas" Jack Skellington, the pumpkin king of Halloween Town, has grown bored with his lot in life and the repetitive nature of giving people a scare each Halloween. A chance visit to neighbouring Christmas Town provides Skellington with a tantalising prospect: why not kidnap Santa Claus and by taking over Santa's duties, administer Christmas instead of Halloween.

But his well-meaning mission to spread Christmas joy to the world unwittingly puts Santa Claus in jeopardy and creates a nightmare for all good little girls and boys every where. At this moment, Jack realizes what was wrong and rescues Santa to make Christmas as it was.

1. I Don't Want to Be Patient.

SCORE |

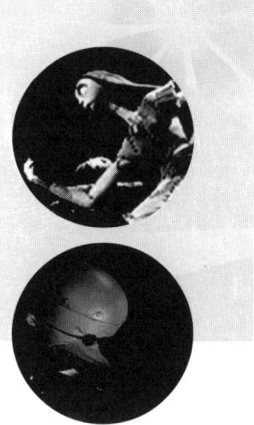

... **Dr. Finkelstein :**

The ¹_____ nightshade you slipped ²_____ wore

³_____ , Sally.

... **Sally :**

Let go!

... **Dr. Finkelstein :**

You're not ⁴_____ for so much ⁵_____ !

... **Sally :**

⁶_____ I am!

... **Dr. Finkelstein :**

You're ⁷_____ with me!

... **Sally :**

Oh no, I'm ⁸_____ !

... **Dr. Finkelstein :**

Come ⁹_____ here you ¹⁰_____ . Oaf! Ow!

... **Dr. Finkelstein :**

Sally, you've ¹¹_____ ¹²_____ .

... **Sally :**

I had to.

... **Dr. Finkelstein :**

For ¹³_____ ?

... **Sally :**

Yes.

... **Dr. Finkelstein :**

Shall we ¹⁴_____ . ~ ~ That's ¹⁵_____ this month you've ¹⁶_____ deadly nightshade ¹⁷_____ my ¹⁸_____ and run ¹⁹_____ —

... **Sally :**

Three ²⁰_____ !

... **Dr. Finkelstein :**

You're ²¹_____ you ²²_____ ! I ²³_____ you ²⁴_____ my ²⁵_____ hands.

... **Sally** :

You ²⁶_____ make ²⁷_____ creations. I'm restless, I can't ²⁸_____ it.

... **Dr. Finkelstein** :

It's ²⁹_____ phase my ³⁰_____ . It'll ³¹_____ .
We need to be ³²_____ . That's ³³_____ .

... **Sally** :

But, I ³⁴_____ want to be ³⁵_____ .

— **EXAMPLEs** —

a   all   away   back   can   come   coming   deadly   dear   don't
excitement   foolish   help   into   know   made   me   mine   not   off
other   own   pass   patient   ready   slipped   tea   then   this   times
twice   with   yes

WORDs and IDIOMs

- nightshade [náitʃèid] : n. 가지속의 식물
- slip [slip] : vt. 살짝 넣다, 살짝 꺼내다
- oaf [ouf] : n. 바보, 멍청이, 바꾸어 놓은 아이
- ow [au] : int. 앗! 아파
- deadly [dédli] : a. 치명적인

- creation [kriːéiʃən] : n. 창조물
- restless [réstlis] : a. 불안한, 쉬지 못하게 하는
- phase [feiz] : n. (변화나 발달의) 단계, 현상
- patient [péiʃənt] : a. 인내심 있는, 참을성 있는

2. Don't Be Silly.

SCORE |

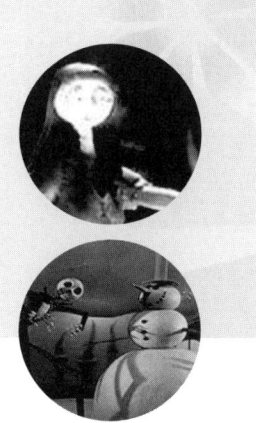

... **Sally :**

Frog's ¹_____ will ²_____ any odor. (Coughing) Bitter. Worm's wart. Where's ³_____ worm's ⁴_____ ?

... **Dr. Finkelstein :**

Sally, that ⁵_____ ready ⁶_____ ?

... **Sally :**

⁷_____ ... lunch.

... **Dr. Finkelstein :**

Ah, what's ⁸_____ ? Worm's ⁹_____ , mmm, and ... frog's ¹⁰_____ .

... **Sally :**

What's ¹¹_____ ? I - I ¹²_____ you liked frog's ¹³_____ .

... **Dr. Finkelstein :**

Nothing's more ¹⁴_____ than frog's ¹⁵_____ .

THE NIGHTMARE BEFORE CHRISTMAS

Until you ⁱ⁶_____ it I ¹⁷_____ swallow a ¹⁸_____ .

... **Sally :**

I'm not ¹⁹_____ ... Oops!

... **Dr. Finkelstein :**

You ²⁰_____ me to ²¹_____ . An old ²²_____ like me ²³_____ hardly has ²⁴_____ as ²⁵_____ is. Me, to ²⁶_____ you ²⁷_____ your very ²⁸_____ .

... **Sally :**

Oh ²⁹_____ be ³⁰_____ . Mmmm ... See. Scrumptious.

EXAMPLEs

breath   coming   don't   hungry   it   life   man   overpower   owe   silly
soup   spoonful   starve   strength   suspicious   taste   that   thought
want   wart   who   whom   wrong   yet

WORDs and IDIOMs

- overpower [òəuvərpáuər] : vt. 압도하다, 이기다
- bitter [bítər] : a. 쓴
- worm [wərm] : n. 벌레, 연충
- wart [wɔːrt] : n. 사마귀, 쥐젖, 나무의 혹
- suspicious [səspíʃəs] : a. 의심스러운, 의심 많은

72 LEARNING ENGLISH WITH ANIMATIONS

- starve [staːrv] : vi. 굶주리다
- strength [streŋθ] : n. 힘, 체력
- silly [síli] : a. 지각없는, 어리석은
- scrumptious [skrʌ́mpʃəs] : a. 굉장히 맛있는, 훌륭한

3. It's a Mistake.

SCORE

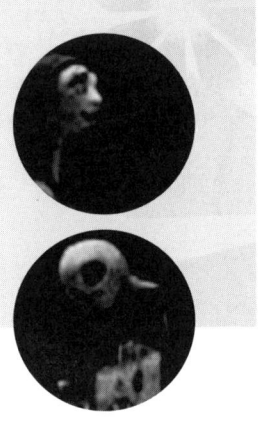

... **Jack :**

Fantastic! Now ¹_____ don't you all ²_____ on ³_____ and we'll be in great ⁴_____. Sally, I ⁵_____ your ⁶_____ more than ⁷_____.

... **Sally :**

You ⁸_____ do, Jack. I had ⁹_____ most ¹⁰_____ vision.

... **Jack :**

That's ¹¹_____.

... **Sally :**

¹²_____, it was ¹³_____ your Xmas. ¹⁴_____ was ¹⁵_____ and ¹⁶_____.

... **Jack :**

That's not ¹⁷_____ Xmas. ¹⁸_____ Xmas is ¹⁹_____ with

20_____ and 21_____ and 22_____ – 23_____ Sandy Claws 24_____ . I want 25_____ to 26_____ 27_____ .

... **Sally :**

Jack, please, 28_____ to 29_____ – it's 30_____ to be a 31_____ .

... **Jack :**

How 32_____ it 33_____ – 34_____ follow the 35_____ . This 36_____ is 37_____ , the trim is 38_____ .

... **Sally :**

39_____ a 40_____ , Jack.

... **Jack :**

Now 41_____ be 42_____ , who 43_____ is 44_____ 45_____ to make 46_____ Sandy Claws outfit.

... **Mayor :**

47_____ !

... **Jack :**

I have 48_____ confidence 49_____ you.

... Sally :

But ⁵⁰_____ seems ⁵¹_____ to ⁵²_____ , very

⁵³_____ .

EXAMPLEs

about   anyone's   be   certainly   clever   could   disaster   don't   else
enough   every   filled   fire   going   help   in   it   it's   joy   just   laugh
listen   make   me   mistake   modest   my   need   next   no   outfit   part
pattern   practice   red   shape   smoke   splendid   terrible   that   the
there   this   white   why   wrong   you

WORDs and IDIOMs

- certainly [sə́:rtənli] : ad. 물론이오, 좋고 말고요
- splendid [spléndid] : a. 훌륭한, 멋진, 근사한, 더할 나위 없는
- outfit [áutfit] : n. 의상, 옷차림
- disaster [dizǽstər] : n. 큰 실패, 큰 불행, 재난
- pattern [pǽtərn] : n. 도안, 무늬, 견본
- modest [mɑ́dist] : a. 겸손한

4. I'm Afraid I'm Not His Type.

SCORE

… **Sally** :

¹_____ Jack, ²_____ !

… **Jack** :

ho ho ha ha ha….

… **Sally** :

Good ³_____ Jack, my ⁴_____ Jack. Oh how I

⁵_____ my premonition is ⁶_____ .

(Sally's Song)

I ⁷_____ there's ⁸_____ in the ⁹_____

That ¹⁰_____ like tragedy's at ¹¹_____ .

And though I'd ¹²_____ to ¹³_____ by him,

Can't ¹⁴_____ this ¹⁵_____ that I ¹⁶_____ !

The ¹⁷_____ is just around the ¹⁸_____ .

And does he ¹⁹_____ my ²⁰_____ for him?

And ²¹_____ he see how ²²_____ he ²³_____ to me?

I think it's ²⁴_____ to be.

What will ²⁵_____ of my ²⁶_____ friend?

Where will his ²⁷_____ lead us ²⁸_____ ?

Although I'd ²⁹_____ to join the ³⁰_____

In their ³¹_____ ³²_____ ,

³³_____ as I may, it doesn't ³⁴_____ .

And will we ³⁵_____ end up ³⁶_____ ?

No, I think not, ³⁷_____ never to ³⁸_____ .

³⁹_____ I am not the ⁴⁰_____ .

EXAMPLEs

actions become bend bye cloud crowd dear dearest enthusiastic
ever feeling feelings feels for hand have hope it's last like
means much no not notice one sense shake something stand
then together try wait will wind worst wrong

WORDs and IDIOMs

- dearest [díərist] : at. 가장 소중한
- shake [ʃeik] : vt. 떨쳐 버리다
- notice [nóutis] : v. ~을 알아채다
- crowd [kraud] : n. 군중, 패거리, 일당
- enthusiastic [inθù:ziǽstik] : a. 열광적인, 열렬한

5. I Wanted to Help You.

SCORE

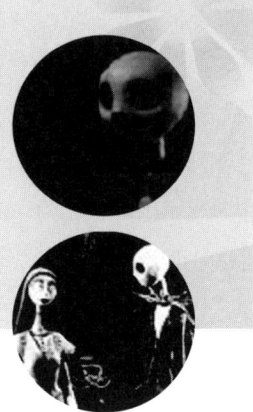

... **Jack :**

¹____ me Mr. Claws. I'm ²____ I've made a ³____ mess of your ⁴____ .

... **Sandy Claws :**

Bumpy sleigh ride, Jack? The ⁵____ time you ⁶____ the urge to take ⁷____ someone else's ⁸____ , I'd ⁹____ to her! She's the ¹⁰____ one who ¹¹____ any ¹²____ around this ¹³____ asylum! Skeletons....

... **Jack :**

I ¹⁴____ there's still ¹⁵____ –

... **Sandy Claws :**

To ¹⁶____ Xmas? Of ¹⁷____ ¹⁸____ is. I'm Santa Claus!

... **Sally :**

He'll 19_____ things Jack. He 20_____ what to 21_____ .

... **Jack :**

22_____ did you get 23_____ here, Sally?

... **Sally :**

Oh, I was 24_____ to, well, I 25_____ to, to –

... **Jack :**

To 26_____ me

... **Sally :**

I couldn't just 27_____ you just…

... **Jack :**

Sally, I can't 28_____ I never 29_____ … that you …

... **Barrel & Lock :**

Jack, Jack!

... **Barrel :**

30_____ he is!

... **Lock :**

31_____ !

… **Shock** :

Just ³²_____ we ³³_____ .

… **Mayor** :

Grab a hold my ³⁴_____ .

… **Jack & Sally** :

Whoa!

EXAMPLEs

afraid   alive   believe   boy   course   do   down   fix   forgive   get   help
here   holiday   hope   how   insane   knows   let   like   listen   makes
next   only   over   realized   said   sense   terrible   there   time   trying
wanted

WORDs and IDIOMs

- mess [mes] : n. 혼란, 난잡
- insane [inséin] : a. 비정상적인, 광기의, 미친 것 같은
- asylum [əsáiləm] : n. 수용소, 은신처, 피난처
- fix [fiks] : vt. 조정하다, 고치다
- realize [ríːəlàiz] : vt. 깨닫다, 자각하다
- alive [əláiv] : a. 살아있는
- grab [græb] : vt. ~을 잡아채다, 움켜쥐다
- gold [gould] : n. 장악, 파악, 이해력
- Whoa! [wou] : inter. (말을 멈추게 할 때 하는 소리) 워!

Mulan ...1998

Summary...... In ancient China when the Mongolian Huns invade China, one man from each family is ordered to join the army and fight. Mulan disguises herself as a man and takes her aging father's place. With the aid of Mushu, a servant to the many guardians that protect the Fa family, Mulan trains hard at the war camp. It is there that she meets Shang, a young captain in the Chinese army.

Mulan becomes a fine soldier when her battalion is called to join the front lines. After travelling high into the snow-covered mountains, the battalion is attacked by Huns. Mulan saves the day by aiming a rocket at the peak, sending an avalanche crushing down on the Huns. Mulan is wounded in the avalanche, however, and falls unconscious. When the doctor examines her, her true nature is finally revealed. Disgraced, she is cast out of the battalion by Shang, who spares her life because she saved theirs.

Mulan and Mushu, lamenting the fact that they must return home without having restored the Fa family's honor, Mulan then witnesses the survival of a small band of Huns, and overhears their plot to assassinate the Emperor. Mulan races off to Imperial City to warn him. When she arrives, she watches in horror as one of Huns captures the Emperor and holds a sword to his throat. Mulan, along with Shang and her three soldier friends, manages to stop Shan Yu and save the Emperor's life. Mulan then returns home, her family's honor restored.

1. Uphold the Family Honor.

SCORE |

… **Mulan** :

Quiet and demure… ¹_____ … ²_____ … delicate …

³_____ … poised … ⁴_____ .

… **Fa Zhou** :

Honorable ⁵_____ , please help Mulan ⁶_____ the

matchmaker ⁷_____ . Please, please, ⁸_____ her.

… **Mulan** :

Father I ⁹_____ your – whoop!

… **Fa Zhou** :

Mulan –

… **Mulan** :

I ¹⁰_____ a spare.

… **Fa Zhou** :

Mulan –

... **Mulan :**

Remember, the ¹¹_____ said three cups of tea in the

¹²_____ .

... **Fa Zhou :**

Mulan–

... **Mulan :**

And three at ¹³_____ .

... **Fa Zhou :**

Mulan, you should ¹⁴_____ be in town. We're ¹⁵_____ on

you to up ...

... **Mulan :**

... uphold the family ¹⁶_____ . Don't worry ¹⁷_____ .

I won't let you ¹⁸_____ . Wish me ¹⁹_____ .

... **Fa Zhou :**

Hurry! I'm ²⁰_____ to ... pray ²¹_____ more.

EXAMPLEs

already   ancestors   brought   counting   doctor   down   father   going
graceful   help   honor   impress   luck   matchmaker   morning   polite
punctual   quiet   refined   some

WORDs and IDIOMs

- whoop [hu:p] : n. (환성) 와! 야!
- spare [spɛər] : n. 비상 준비품
- uphold [ʌphóuld] : vt. 올리다
- pray [prei] : vt. 빌다, 기원하다
- quiet [kwáiət] : a. 조용한, 정숙한, 얌전한, 말수가 적은
- demure [dimjúər] : a. 품위 있는, 침착한, 착실한
- graceful [gréisfəl] : a. 우아한, 기품 있는, 단아한
- delicate [délikit] : a. 섬세한, 자상한
- polite [pəláit] : a. 공손한, 예절바른
- refined [rifáind] : a. 세련된, 품위 있는
- poised [pɔizd] : a. 균형 잡힌
- honorable [únərəbl] : a. 훌륭한, 고귀한
- punctual [pʌ́ŋktʃuəl] : a. 시간을 지키는, 늦지 않는
- ancestors [ǽnsestər] : n. 조상, 선조
- impress [imprés] : vt. ~의 마음을 흔들다, ~에게 감명을 주다, ~을 인상지우다
- matchmaker [mǽtʃmeikər] : n. 중매쟁이
- honor [ánər] : n. 명예, 체면
- uphold [ʌphóuld] : v. (전통, 명성)을 유지하다, 지지하다

2. Men Want Girls

SCORE

... **Fa Li and Others :**

A ⁱ_____ can bring her ²_____ great ³_____ in one way by striking a good ⁴_____ . And ⁵_____ could be the ⁶_____ .

... **Dresser 1 :**

Men ⁷_____ girls with good ⁸_____ .

... **Dresser 2 :**

Calm.

... **Fa Li :**

⁹_____ .

... **Dresser 1 :**

Who work fast– ¹⁰_____ .

... **Fa Li :**

With good ¹¹_____ .

... **Dresser 2** :

And a ¹²_____ waist.

EXAMPLEs

breeding   day   family   girl   honor   match   obedient   paced   taste
this   waist   want

WORDs and IDIOMs

- strike [straik] : vt. ~에 인상을 심다
- taste [teist] : n. 미각, 입맛
- obedient [obí:diənt] : a. 순종하는, 양순한
- paced [peist] : a. ~걸음의
- breeding [brí:diŋ] : n. 양육, 예의범절
- tiny [táini] : a. 자그마한

3. Will Never Bring Your Family Honor?

SCORE

... **Matchmaker** :

Huh, Hmm, too ¹_____ . Hmph, not ²_____ for bearing ³_____ . ⁴_____ the ⁵_____ admonition.

... **Mulan** :

Mmm-Hmm. Ptu.

... **Matchmaker** :

Well...

... **Mulan** :

Fulfill your ⁶_____ calmly and re ... – spectfully. ⁷_____ before ⁸_____ snack ⁹_____ . This ¹⁰_____ bring ¹¹_____ honor and glory.

... **Matchmaker** :

Hmmm, ¹²_____ way. ¹³_____ , pour the ¹⁴_____ . To ¹⁵_____ your ¹⁶_____ in – ¹⁷_____ you ¹⁸_____

¹⁹_____ a ²⁰_____ of dignity and ²¹_____ .

You ²²_____ also ²³_____ poised.

… **Mulan :**

Um, ²⁴_____ me.

… **Matchmaker :**

And ²⁵_____ !

… **Mulan :**

Could I ²⁶_____ take that ²⁷_____ … one ²⁸_____ .

… **Matchmaker :**

²⁹_____ you ³⁰_____ – Wooo, woooo, wooooooo, Ahhhhhhhhhhh ~ ~ ~ ~ ~

… **Grandma Fa :**

I ³¹_____ it's ³²_____ ³³_____ , don't ³⁴_____ ?

… **Matchmaker :**

Put it ³⁵_____ ! Put it ³⁶_____ ! ³⁷_____ it ³⁸_____ !

³⁹_____ are a ⁴⁰_____ ! You ⁴¹_____ look ⁴²_____ a ⁴³_____ , but you ⁴⁴_____ never ⁴⁵_____ your ⁴⁶_____ ⁴⁷_____ !

EXAMPLEs

act back be bride bring clumsy demonstrate disgrace duties
family final future going good honor just laws like may
moment must now out pardon please put recite refinement
reflect sense shall silent skinny sons tea think this well why
will you

WORDs and IDIOMs

- skinny [skíni] : a. 말라빠진, 피골이 상접한
- recite [risáit] : vt. ~을 암송하다
- bear [bɛər] : vt. ~을 낳다
- admonition [æ̀dməníʃən] : n. 훈계, 충고
- fulfill [fulfíl] : vt. ~을 이행하다, 실행하다
- demonstrate [démənstrèit] : vt. 설명하다
- refinement [rifáinmənt] : n. 고상, 고아
- clumsy [klʌ́mzi] : a. 얼빠진, 눈치 없는, 서투른

4. Reflection.

SCORE |

... **Mulan :**

Look ¹____ ²____ I ³____ ⁴____ pass ⁵____ a ⁶____ bride or a ⁷____ daughter. ⁸____ it ⁹____ ¹⁰____ not ¹¹____ to ¹²____ this ¹³____ ? ¹⁴____ I ¹⁵____ ¹⁶____ if I ¹⁷____ to truly to ¹⁸____ ¹⁹____ , I ²⁰____ ²¹____ my family's ²²____ .

²³____ is that ²⁴____ I ²⁵____ staring ²⁶____ ²⁷____ at ²⁸____ ? ²⁹____ is my ³⁰____ ³¹____ I ³²____ ³³____ ? ³⁴____ I ³⁵____ ³⁶____ who ³⁷____ ³⁸____ though I've ³⁹____ . ⁴⁰____ ⁴¹____ my reflection ⁴²____ ⁴³____ I ⁴⁴____ ⁴⁵____ ?

⁴⁶_____ ⁴⁷_____ my ⁴⁸_____ show ⁴⁹_____ I ⁵⁰_____ ⁵¹_____ ?

... Fa Zhou :

Umhum. My, my, ⁵²_____ beautiful ⁵³_____ we have ⁵⁴_____ ⁵⁵_____ . But ⁵⁶_____ , ⁵⁷_____ one's ⁵⁸_____ . But I'll ⁵⁹_____ that ⁶⁰_____ it ⁶¹_____ , it will ⁶²_____ the ⁶³_____ beautiful of ⁶⁴_____ .

EXAMPLEs

all   am   at   back   be   bet   blooms   blossoms   break   can   cannot
don't   for   girl   heart   hide   I   I'm   inside   know   late   look   me
meant   most   myself   never   now   part   perfect   play   reflection   see
show   somehow   someone   straight   that   this   tried   were   what
when   who   why   will   would   year

WORDs and IDIOMs

- perfect [pə́ːrfikt] : a. 완벽한, 더할 나위 없는
- break [breik] : vt. 찢다, 상처 나게 하다
- reflection [riflékʃən] : n. 반성, 숙고
- blossom [blásəm] : n. 꽃, 개화, 청춘
- bet [bet] : vt. 내기를 하다

*I bet ~ : ~이라고 생각하다 / I bet you ~ : 틀림없이 ~ 이다
- bloom [blu:m] : vi. 꽃이 피다

5. A Girl Worth Fighting for.

SCORE |

... **Army Chorus :**

For a long 1_____ we've been marching off the 2_____ .

... **Yao :**

In a thundering 3_____ we feel a lot like 4_____ .

... **Cow :**

Moo

... **Army Chorus :**

Like the pounding beat our aching 5_____ aren't easy to

6_____ .

... **Ling :**

Hey, think of instead, a 7_____ worth 8_____ for.

... **Mulan :**

Huh?

... **Ling :**

That's what I said, a ⁹_____ worth ¹⁰_____ for. I ¹¹_____ her paler than the ¹²_____ with eyes that shine like ¹³_____ .

... **Yao :**

My girl will marvel at my ¹⁴_____ , ¹⁵_____ my battle ¹⁶_____ . I couldn't care less what she'll ¹⁷_____ or what she ¹⁸_____ like. It all depends on what she ¹⁹_____ like beef, pork, chicken…

... **Mulan :**

Uh, how about a girl who's got a ²⁰_____ ? Who ²¹_____ speaks her ²²_____ ?

... **Ling, Yao and Chien-Po :**

Nah!

EXAMPLEs

adore battle brain cattle cooks feet fighting girl herd ignore long looks mind moon paler scars speaks stars strength want wear

 **WORDs and IDIOMs**

- herd [həːrd] : n. 군중, 평민
- ache [eik] : vi. 아프다, 쑤시다, ~을 멸망하다
- worth [wəːrθ] : a. ~이 할 가치가 있는
- pale [peil] : adj. 창백한, 안색에 핏기가 없는
- marvel [máːrvəl] : vt. 경탄하다, ~에 놀라다
- adore [ədɔ́ːr] : vt. ~을 숭배하다, ~을 무척 좋아하다
- scar [skɑːr] : n. 흉터, 자국
- brain [brein] : n. 지력, 두뇌

6. Flower Blooms in Adversity.

SCORE

... **Emperor :**

I'v heard a great ¹_____ about you, Fa ²_____ . You ³_____ your father's ⁴_____ , ran away ⁵_____ home, impersonated a ⁶_____ , deceived your commanding ⁷_____ , dishonored the Chinese ⁸_____ , destroyed my palace. And ... you have ⁹_____ us all. Chi Fu!

... **Chi Fu :**

¹⁰_____ Excellency?

... **Emperor :**

See to it that this ¹¹_____ is made a ¹²_____ of my council. The ¹³_____ that blooms in ¹⁴_____ is the most ¹⁵_____ and beautiful of all.

... **Shang :**

Sir?

MULAN 99

... **Emperor** :

You don't ¹⁶_____ ___ a girl like that ev'ry ¹⁷_____ .

EXAMPLEs

adversity armor army deal dynasty flower from meet member
Mulan officer rare saved soldier stole woman your

WORDs and IDIOMs

- armor [ɑ́:rmər] : n. 갑옷과 투구
- commanding [kəmǽndiŋ] : adj. 지휘하는, 명령하는
- officer [ɔ́:fisər] : n. 장교, 사관
    *commanding officer : 부대 지휘관, 부대장
- impersonate [impə́:rsənèit] : vt. ~인 체하다, ~을 흉내 내다
- deceive [disí:v] : vt. ~을 속이다, 기만하다
- council [káunsəl] : n. 자문 위원회, 평의회
- adversity [ædvə́:rsiti] : n. 역경, 재앙
- rare [rɛə:r] : adj. 진기한, 훌륭한
- dynasty [dáinəsti] : n. 왕조

Shrek ...2001

Summary...... Once upon a time, in a far away swamp, there lived a big green ogre named Shrek. In a nearby kingdom, Lord Farquaad decides to expel all the fairy tale creatures from his kingdom, and Shrek is horrified to find out that the creatures have been dumped off in his swamp. Shrek, determined to save their home, cuts a deal with Farquaad and sets out to rescue the beautiful Princess Fiona to be Farquaad's bride. Accompanying him on his mission is wisecracking Donkey.

However, rescuing the Princess from a fire-breathing dragon may prove the least of their problems when the deep, dark secret she has been keeping is revealed. When they come back to home, it turned out that the Fiona was an ogre too. Finally Shrek and Fiona married and lived on the swamp with donkey while characters back to their land.

1. She Waited Her True Love.

SCORE

Once upon a ¹_____ there was a ²_____ princess. But she had an ³_____ upon her of fearful ⁴_____, which could only be ⁵_____ by love's ⁶_____ kiss. She was ⁷_____ away in a ⁸_____ guarded by a terrible fire breathing ⁹_____. Many ¹⁰_____ knights had attempted to ¹¹_____ her from this dreadful ¹²_____, but none prevailed. She waited in the dragon's ¹³_____ in the ¹⁴_____ room of the tallest ¹⁵_____ for her true love and ¹⁶_____ love's first kiss.

EXAMPLEs

brave   broken   castle   dragon   enchantment   first   free   highest   keep
locked   lovely   prison   room   sort   time   tower   true

SHREK 103

 **WORDs and IDIOMs**

- enchantment [intʃǽntmənt] : n. 마법에 걸린 상태, 마법을 걸기
- guarded [gɑ:rdid] : a. 감시를 받는
- breath [brí:ðiŋ] : a. 숨을 내쉬는, 토해내는
- brave [breiv] : a. 용감한, 멋진
- knight [nait] : n. 기사
- dreadful [drédfəl] : a. 무시무시한, 무서운
- prevail [privéil] : vi. 승리하다, 이기다
- tower [táuə:r] : n. 탑

2. Unexpected Encounter.

SCORE

... **Shrek :**

¹_____ up!

... **Princess Fiona :**

What?

... **Shrek :**

Are you ²_____ Fiona?

... **Princess Fiona :**

I am. Awaiting a ³_____ so bold as to ⁴_____ me.

... **Shrek :**

Oh, that's ⁵_____ . Now let's ⁶_____ .

... **Princess Fiona :**

But ⁷_____ , Sir knight. This be our ⁸_____ meeting.

Should it not be ⁹_____ , romantic moment?

... **Shrek :**

Yeah. Sorry 10_____ , there's no 11_____ .

... **Princess Fiona :**

Hey, wait. 12_____ are you 13_____ ? You know, you 14_____ sweep me off my 15_____ out yonder 16_____ and down a 17_____ onto your valiant steed.

... **Shrek :**

You've had a lot of 18_____ to plan this, 19_____ you?

... **Princess Fiona :**

Mm-hmm... But we 20_____ to savor through this 21_____ . You 22_____ recite an epic poem for me. A ballad, a sonnet, a limerick. Or 23_____ .

... **Shrek :**

I don't think 24_____ .

... **Princess Fiona :**

Well, 25_____ I at least know the 26_____ of 27_____ champion?

... **Shrek :**

Um, Shrek.

... **Princess Fiona :**

Sir Shrek, I pray that you 28_____ this favor as a 29_____ of my gratitude.

... **Shrek :**

Thanks.

(Roaring)

... **Princess Fiona :**

You didn't 30_____ the dragon?

... **Shrek :**

It's not my to do this. Now, come on!

... **Princess Fiona :**

But this isn't 31_____ . You were meant to 32_____ in sword, drawn, banner flying. That's what all the other 33_____ did.

... **Shrek :**

Yeah, right 34_____ they burst in the flame.

... **Princess Fiona :**

That's not the 35_____ . Oh, wait. Where are you 36_____ ?

Exit is over there.

... **Shrek :**

Well, I have to ⁣³⁷_____ my ass.

... **Princess Fiona :**

What ³⁸_____ of ³⁹_____ are you?

... **Shrek :**

One of a ⁴⁰_____ .

EXAMPLEs

before   can   charge   could   doing   feet   first   go   going   have
haven't   kind   knight   lady   moment   my   name   nice   point   princess
rescue   right   rope   save   should   slay   so   something   taken   time
token   wait   wake   what   window   wonderful

WORDs and IDIOMs

- bold [bould] : a. 대담한
- rescue [réskju] : vt. 구하다, 구출하다
- sweep [swi:p] : vt. 공손히 절을 하다, 몰아가다
    *sweep a person of his/her feet : 한눈에 반하게 하다
- yonder [jándər] : a. 저쪽의
- valiant [væljənt] : a. 용감한, 씩씩한
- steed [sti:d] : n. 군마

- savor [séivər] : vt. 맛보다, 완미하다
- recite [risáit] : vt. ~을 낭송하다, 암송하다
- epic [épik] : n. 서사시
- balled [bǽləd] : n. 민요
- sonnet [sánit] : n. 소넷, 14행 시
- limerick [límərik] : n. 오행 속요
- champion [tʃǽmpiən] : n. 우승자
- favor [féivər] : n. 호의, 친절
- gratitude [grǽtətùːd] : n. 감사, 사의
- ballade [bæláːd] : n. 발라드, 서사곡
- charge [tʃɑːrdʒ] : vt. 돌격하다, 돌진하다
- drawn [drɔːn] : a. 칼집에서 빼낸
- banner [bǽnər] : n. 기
- burst [bəːrst] : vt. 폭발하다, 터지다
- flame [fleim] : n. 불꽃, 불길

3. Not a Price, but an Ogar.

SCORE

... **Princess Fiona :**

The ¹_____ is won. You may remove your ²_____ good Sir Knight.

... **Shrek :**

A, no.

... **Princess Fiona :**

³_____ not?

... **Shrek :**

I, I have ⁴_____ hair.

... **Princess Fiona :**

Please. I wouldst look ⁵_____ the face of my rescuer.

... **Shrek :**

No, no, ⁶_____ wouldn't, dust.

... **Princess Fiona :**

But, ⁷_____ will you kiss ⁸_____ ?

... **Shrek :**

What? That wasn't in a ⁹_____ description.

... **Donkey :**

¹⁰_____ it's a perk?

... **Princess Fiona :**

No. It's ¹¹_____ . You must know ¹²_____ it goes. A princess

locked in a ¹³_____ and beset by a dragon is rescued by a

¹⁴_____ knight. And then they share ¹⁵_____ love's first kiss.

... **Donkey :**

With Shrek? You think, ¹⁶_____ ... you think Shrek is your

¹⁷_____ love?

... **Princess Fiona :**

Well, yes.

... **Donkey :**

Aha, ha ha ~ ~ . You think Shrek is your true love.

... **Princess Fiona :**

What is so ¹⁸_____ ?

... **Shrek :**

Let's just say, I'm ¹⁹_____ your type, ok?

... **Princess Fiona :**

Of ²⁰_____ you are. You're my ²¹_____ . Now, now remove your ²²_____ .

... **Shrek :**

Look. I ²³_____ don't think this is a ²⁴_____ idea.

... **Princess Fiona :**

Just take ²⁵_____ the helmet.

... **Shrek :**

I'm not ²⁶_____ to.

... **Princess Fiona :**

Take it ²⁷_____ !

... **Shrek :**

No!

... **Princess Fiona :**

Now!

... **Shrek :**

Ok, ²⁸_____ . ²⁹_____ you command, your ³⁰_____ .

112 LEARNING ENGLISH WITH ANIMATIONS

... **Princess Fiona :**

You ... You're an Ogre.

... **Shrek :**

Oh, you were ⁳¹_____ prince Charming.

... **Princess Fiona :**

Well, yes ³²_____ . No. This is ³³_____ wrong. You're not ³⁴_____ to be an Ogre.

EXAMPLEs

actually all as battle brave course destiny easy expecting
funny going good helmet highness how job maybe me not
off really rescuer supposed tower true upon wait why you

WORDs and IDIOMs

- battle [bǽtl] : n. 전투, 싸움
- helmet [hélmit] : n. 투구
- perk [pəːrk] : n. 임시수입, 팁, 특전
- destiny [déstəni] : n. 운명
- beset [bisét] : vt. 포위하다, 에워싸다
- funny [fʌ́ni] : a. 우스운
- rescuer [réskuːər] : n. 구원자
- remove [rimúːv] : vt. 벗다

- command [kʌmǽnd] : vt. ~에게 명령하다, 요구하다
- highness [háinis] : n. 전하
- actually [ǽktʃuəli] : ad. 정말로 (강조 또는 놀람을 나타냄)
- suppose [səpóuz] : vt. 추측하다, 생각하다   *be supposed to ~ : ~할 것으로 기대되다

ANSWERs

Snow White

Who is the Fairest of All?

1. mirror	2. wall	3. fairest
4. beauty	5. But	6. see
7. hide	8. grace	9. she
10. fair	11. thee	12. Alas
13. Reveal	14. name	15. Lips
16. rose	17. hair	18. black
19. Skin	20. snow	21. White

I'll Keep House for You.

1. shut	2. her	3. get
4. don't	5. away	6. if
7. kill	8. kill	9. stepmother
10. queen	11. witch	12. finds
13. down	14. know	15. am
16. knows	17. everything	18. magic
19. can	20. make	21. invisible
22. be	23. room	24. now
25. never	26. me	27. me
28. keep	29. wash	30. sweep
31. cook	32. you	33. Apple
34. Yes	35. pie	36. she
37. soup	38. minute	39. not
40. ready	41. have	42. wash

A Love Story.

1. story	2. us	3. story
4. true	5. love	6. once

7. the	8. fell	9. could
10. charming	11. one	12. strong
13. big	14. tall	15. nobody
16. all	17. say	18. steal
19. romantic	20. not	21. prince
22. someday	23. meet	24. castle
25. forever		

Magic Wishing Apple.

1. good	2. old	3. secret
4. ordinary	5. magic	6. apple
7. apple	8. bite	9. dreams
10. true	11. make	12. take
13. something	14. desires	15. someone
16. love	17. someone	18. thought
19. so	20. knows	21. heart
22. take	23. wish	24. wish
25. go	26. on	27. carry
28. castle	29. live	30. after
31. bite	32. cold	33. strange

Sleeping Beauty

A Princess Was Born.

1. far	2. land	3. ago
4. king	5. fair	6. years
7. they	8. for	9. child
10. finally	11. wish	12. daughter
13. born	14. called	15. they

16. after	17. dawn	18. lives
19. sunshine	20. great	21. holiday
22. throughout	23. kingdom	24. all
25. high	26. estate	27. pay
28. to	29. infant	

Three Gifts.

1. most	2. and	3. excellencies
4. three	5. good	6. Mistress
7. and	8. the	9. darling
10. your	11. us	12. child
13. bless	14. single	15. more
16. less	17. princess	18. gift
19. be	20. gift	21. beauty
22. beauty	23. sunshine	24. red
25. rose	26. she	27. tiny
28. gift	29. shall	30. gift
31. gift	32. song	33. Sweet
34. my	35. gift	

She Will Die.

1. she	2. here	3. quite
4. king	5. royalty	6. gentry
7. how	8. even	9. really
10. not	11. receiving	12. invitation
13. dear	14. awkward	15. situation
16. it	17. oversight	18. way
19. not	20. excellency	21. majesty
22. show	23. will	24. shall
25. gift	26. child	27. well
28. you	29. princess	30. grow
31. grace	32. beauty	33. by
34. know	35. but	36. before

37. sets	38. birthday	39. shall
40. finger	41. on	42. wheel
43. die	44. no	45. creature
46. back	47. fool	

Not in Death, but in Sleep.

1. despair	2. has	3. gift
4. give	5. she	6. this
7. curse	8. no	9. far
10. great	11. she	12. help
13. do	14. best	15. princess
16. wicked	17. a	18. finger
19. hope	20. still	21. in
22. gift	23. in	24. sleep
25. keep	26. from	27. shall
28. wake	29. spell	30. break
31. all		

The Little Mermaid

He's So Handsome.

1. seen	2. human	3. close
4. before	5. handsome	6. isn't
7. hairy	8. to	9. that
10. playing	11. alone	12. entire
13. wants	14. you	15. happily
16. down	17. out	18. somewhere
19. just	20. just	21. found

22. you	23. looking	24. enough
25. me	26. find	27. hit
28. lightning		

What Would I Give?

1. dead	2. hard	3. say
4. make	5. heartbeat	6. breathing
7. so	8. beautiful	9. What
10. give	11. live	12. what
13. pay	14. stay	15. beside
16. you	17. would	18. see
19. smiling	20. at	21. where
22. could	23. stay	24. sun
25. you	26. me	27. could
28. part	29. world	

I'll Swim to His Castle.

1. loves	2. me	3. not
4. He	5. me	6. knew
7. stop	8. crazy	9. got
10. to	11. tonight	12. where
13. lives	14. will	15. get
16. head	17. clouds	18. in
19. water	20. belongs	21. swim
22. castle	23. splash	24. get
25. attention	26. here	27. home

I Love Him.

1. rescued	2. human	3. drowning
4. I	5. human	6. world
7. forbidden	8. you	9. that

10. knows	11. would	12. died
13. less	14. worry	15. about
16. don't	17. know	18. don't
19. know	20. all	21. same
22. savage	23. fish	24. incapable
25. feeling	26. love	27. him
28. No	29. lost	30. senses
31. He's	32. human	33. You're
34. mermaid	35. I	36. care
37. help	38. going	39. through
40. this	41. the	42. only
43. so	44. No	45. stop
46. Daddy		

Never Be with My Family Again?

1. got	2. deal	3. become
4. human	5. never	6. with
7. father	8. sisters	9. again
10. right	11. But	12. have
13. man	14. Life	15. full
16. choices	17. it	18. and
19. there	20. more	21. Thing
22. we	23. discussed	24. subject
25. payment	26. get	27. something
28. nothing	29. know	30. don't
31. asking	32. token	33. trifle
34. You'll	35. miss	36. it
37. What	38. want	39. you
40. voice	41. voice	42. You
43. got	44. more	45. talking
46. singing	47. without	48. my
49. how	50. have	51. looks
52. pretty	53. face	54. don't
55. importance	56. body	57. language
58. men	59. don't	60. like

61. think   62. gossips   63. land
64. ladies   65. not   66. word

Beauty and the Beast

Bell Is a Funny Girl.

1. morning	2. Good morning	3. you
4. to	5. bookshop	6. finished
7. wonderful	8. about	9. and
10. nice	11. hurry	12. up
13. Look	14. she	15. girl
16. strange	17. question	18. can't
19. tell	20. crowd	21. some
22. she's	23. funny	

Belle's Favorite Book.

1. return	2. borrowed	3. already
4. put	5. got	6. new
7. since	8. That's	9. right
10. borrow	11. this	12. read
13. favorite	14. far	15. magic
16. prince	17. like	18. yours
19. insist	20. thank	21. you
22. very	23. she	24. peculiar
25. feeling	26. dreamy	27. her
28. book	29. a	30. to
31. us		

Different from the Rest of Us.

1. isn't	2. amazing	3. It's
4. favorite	5. because	6. see
7. Here's	8. she	9. prince
10. she	11. discover	12. him
13. three	14. it's	15. wonder
16. that	17. name	18. beauty
19. looks	20. no	21. behind
22. fair	23. afraid	24. odd
25. different	26. rest	27. nothing
28. different	29. rest	30. us

He's Not for Me.

1. did	2. time	3. book
4. odd	5. odd	6. you
7. idea	8. don't	9. sure
10. fit	11. one	12. to
13. about	14. handsome	15. handsome
16. right	17. rude	18. for

There's Something in Him.

1. sweet	2. kind	3. mean
4. and	5. dear	6. unsure
7. why	8. there	9. alarming
10. thought	11. charming	12. something
13. simply		

The Nightmare Before Christmas

I Don't Want to Be Patient.

1. deadly	2. me	3. off
4. ready	5. excitement	6. Yes
7. Coming	8. not	9. back
10. foolish	11. come	12. back
13. this	14. then	15. twice
16. slipped	17. into	18. tea
19. off	20. times	21. mine
22. know	23. made	24. with
25. own	26. can	27. other
28. help	29. a	30. dear
31. pass	32. patient	33. all
34. don't	35. patient	

Don't Be Silly.

1. breath	2. overpower	3. that
4. wart	5. soup	6. yet
7. Coming	8. that	9. wart
10. breath	11. wrong	12. thought
13. breath	14. suspicious	15. breath
16. taste	17. won't	18. spoonful
19. hungry	20. want	21. starve
22. man	23. who	24. strength
25. it	26. whom	27. owe
28. life	29. don't	30. silly

It's a Mistake.

1. why
2. practice
3. that
4. shape
5. need
6. help
7. anyone's
8. certainly
9. the
10. terrible
11. splendid
12. No
13. about
14. There
15. smoke
16. fire
17. my
18. My
19. filled
20. laughs
21. joy
22. this
23. my
24. outfit
25. you
26. make
27. it
28. listen
29. me
30. going
31. disaster
32. could
33. be
34. just
35. pattern
36. part
37. red
38. white
39. It's
40. mistake
41. don't
42. modest
43. else
44. clever
45. enough
46. my
47. Next
48. every
49. in
50. it
51. wrong
52. me
53. wrong

I'm Afraid I'm Not His Type.

1. Wait
2. no
3. bye
4. dearest
5. hope
6. wrong
7. sense
8. something
9. wind
10. feels
11. hand
12. like
13. stand
14. shake
15. feeling
16. have
17. worst
18. bend
19. notice
20. feelings
21. will
22. much
23. means
24. not
25. become
26. dear
27. actions
28. then
29. like
30. crowd
31. enthusiastic
32. cloud
33. Try
34. last
35. ever
36. together
37. it's
38. become
39. For
40. one

I Wanted to Help You.

1. Forgive	2. afraid	3. terrible
4. holiday	5. next	6. get
7. over	8. holiday	9. listen
10. only	11. makes	12. sense
13. insane	14. hope	15. time
16. fix	17. course	18. there
19. fix	20. knows	21. do
22. How	23. down	24. trying
25. wanted	26. help	27. let
28. believe	29. realized	30. Here
31. Alive	32. like	33. said
34. boy		

Mulan

Uphold the Family Honor.

1. graceful	2. polite	3. refined
4. punctual	5. ancestors	6. impress
7. today	8. help	9. brought
10. brought	11. doctor	12. morning
13. night	14. already	15. counting
16. honor	17. father	18. down
19. luck	20. going	21. some

Men Want Girls.

1. girl	2. family	3. honor
4. match	5. this	6. day

7. want 8. taste 9. Obedient
10. paced 11. breeding 12. tiny

Will Never Bring Your Family Honor?

1. skinny 2. good 3. sons
4. Recite 5. final 6. duties
7. Reflect 8. you 9. act
10. shall 11. you 12. this
13. now 14. tea 15. please
16. future 17. laws 18. must
19. demonstrate 20. sense 21. refinement
22. must 23. be 24. pardon
25. silent 26. just 27. back
28. moment 29. Why 30. clumsy
31. think 32. going 33. well
34. you 35. out 36. out
37. put 38. out 39. You
40. disgrace 41. may 42. like
43. bride 44. will 45. bring
46. family 47. honor

Reflection.

1. at 2. me 3. will
4. never 5. for 6. perfect
7. perfect 8. Can 9. be
10. I'm 11. meant 12. play
13. part 14. Now 15. see
16. that 17. were 18. be
19. myself 20. would 21. break
22. heart 23. Who 24. girl
25. see 26. straight 27. back
28. me 29. Why 30. reflection
31. someone 32. don't 33. know

34. Somehow	35. cannot	36. hide
37. I	38. am	39. tried
40. When	41. will	42. show
43. who	44. am	45. inside
46. When	47. will	48. reflection
49. who	50. am	51. inside
52. what	53. blossoms	54. this
55. year	56. look	57. this
58. late	59. bet	60. when
61. blooms	62. be	63. most
64. all		

A Girl Worth Fighting for.

1. time	2. battle	3. herd
4. cattle	5. feet	6. ignore
7. girl	8. fighting	9. girl
10. fighting	11. want	12. moon
13. stars	14. strength	15. adore
16. scars	17. wear	18. looks
19. cooks	20. brain	21. speaks
22. mind		

Flower Blooms in Adversity.

1. deal	2. Mulan	3. stole
4. armor	5. from	6. soldier
7. officer	8. army	9. saved
10. Your	11. woman	12. member
13. flower	14. adversity	15. rare
16. meet	17. dynasty	

Shrek

She Waited Her True Love.

1. time	2. lovely	3. enchantment
4. sort	5. broken	6. first
7. locked	8. castle	9. dragon
10. brave	11. free	12. prison
13. keep	14. highest	15. tower
16. true		

Unexpected Encounter.

1. Wake	2. princess	3. knight
4. rescue	5. nice	6. go
7. wait	8. first	9. wonderful
10. lady	11. time	12. what
13. doing	14. should	15. feet
16. window	17. rope	18. time
19. haven't	20. have	21. moment
22. could	23. something	24. so
25. can	26. name	27. my
28. take	29. token	30. slay
31. right	32. charge	33. knight
34. before	35. point	36. going
37. save	38. kind	39. knight
40. kind		

Not a Price, but an Ogar.

1. battle	2. helmet	3. Why
4. helmet	5. upon	6. you
7. how	8. me	9. job

10. Maybe	11. destiny	12. how
13. tower	14. brave	15. true
16. wait	17. true	18. funny
19. not	20. course	21. rescuer
22. helmet	23. really	24. good
25. off	26. going	27. off
28. easy	29. As	30. highness
31. expecting	32. actually	33. all
34. supposed		

편저자 이영주

서강대학교 영문학과 졸업. 서강대학교 대학원 영문학과 졸업(석사, 박사).
고전 · 르네상스영문학회 편집이사 역임. 한국현대영미드라마학회 총무이사 역임.
현 한국셰익스피어학회 재무이사.
현 장안대학 외국어학부 영어과 교수.

논문 : The Vision of Time in Tennessee Williams' Plays (박사 논문)
"굶주림의 다면적 측면에서 본 『저주의 극빈층』"
"『탬벌레인 대왕』: 르네상스 휴머니즘 정신과 그 딜레마"
"A Moon for the Misbegotten에 나타난 조시의 이중성 해부 : 자전적 측면에서"
"셰익스피어와 르네상스 극에 나타난 남녀 마법사의 재현의 차이와 그 의미"
"Reading Eugene O'Neill's Plays in Film"
"Comic Vision in the Absurd World" 등

저서 : Writing as a Fun, Singing and Learning English, English Conversation Made Easier,
Let's Get Started, Learning English through Movies.

역서 : 『모더니즘과 포스트모더니즘』(공역), 유진 오닐의 『불출들의 달』, 아이스킬로스의 『아가멤논』

만화영화로 배우는 영어

초판2쇄 • 2011년 2월 20일
편저자 • 이영주/ 발행인 • 이성모 / 발행처 • 도서출판 동인
서울시 종로구 명륜동 2가 237 아남주상복합Ⓐ 118호/ 등록 • 제1-1599호
TEL • (02) 765-7145 / FAX • (02) 765-7165 / E-mail • dongin60@chollian.net / Homepage • donginbook.co.kr

ISBN: 89-5506-281-8   13740   정가 • 10,000원